The Color Nature Library
ORCHIDS

By
PETER TAYLOR

Designed and Produced by
TED SMART and DAVID GIBBON

CRESCENT BOOKS

INTRODUCTION

The orchids comprise one of the largest families of flowering plants with about 20,000 known wild species. Botanically they belong to the group known as *Monocotyledons* which includes also the grasses and lilies. The popular conception of orchids being something special and different is based on scientific fact as they are indeed unique in their growth and flower structure, their association with other plants and especially their relationships with pollinating insects. Within the group, although there exists a basically uniform structure, there is an enormous variation in appearance and habit. They vary in size from tiny plants a few centimetres high to giants of many metres. In habit they are of two main types – *terrestrial*, that is growing and rooting in the ground, or *epiphytic*, which means that they grow upon other plants, usually trees, without actually being parasites. The terrestrials are the only kind found in temperate countries, the epiphytes are exclusively tropical, and it is these, or their hybrids, which are the colourful cultivated orchids. Epiphytes attach themselves to their host tree by means of specialised aerial roots through which they absorb nourishment and also moisture from the air. Many of them have inflated stems, called *pseudobulbs* which act as storage organs in periods of drought.

Orchids occur wild in most parts of the world except the very coldest and driest regions but while there are a hundred or so wild in Europe and perhaps twice that number in the United States, it is estimated that 2,000 species occur in Ecuador and 2,300 in Brazil. Only a relatively small number of genera are commonly grown, but by hybridisation both within and between genera over 40,000 cultivated kinds have been named.

What is it that makes the orchids so different from other plants? Firstly perhaps the unique structure of the flowers. As in the lilies there are six floral segments, three outer sepals and three inner petals, but whereas in the lily the six segments are all more or less similar the apparently lower petal of an orchid is markedly dissimilar, usually more colourful and ornamental, and is termed the *lip*. Actually although usually appearing lowermost it is in fact the uppermost petal but the flower stalk and ovary supporting the flower is twisted through 90°. Sometimes the lip is uppermost by a further rotation through the full 360°. In the orchid flower we do not see the six male stamens and the separate female pistil and stigmas of the lily. Instead these are united into a single organ, termed the *column*, which usually bears at its apex a single stamen – an exception is found in the slipper orchids, *Paphiopedilum* and related genera, which have two stamens – and the stigma is usually situated below on the front of the column. The pollen of most orchids is collected into masses termed *pollinia*. These, numbering from two to eight according to species, are contained within the stamen and usually have at the base a sticky disk or *viscidium*.

The lip and the modified sexual parts are the secret of the uniqueness of the orchid flower. The pollinating insect (or sometimes bird or bat) is attracted to the lip in search of some reward. In attempting to obtain this reward, which may be nectar, some particular part of its body comes in contact with the viscidium so that when it withdraws from the flower it does so with one or more pollinia firmly attached. By various ingenious contrivances it is so arranged that on visiting another flower of the same species these pollinia will contact the stigma and so effect fertilization. It is not always nectar that the visitor may be seeking. In some orchids scent and shape of the lip stimulates mating behaviour in certain insects which then remove pollinia in attempting to copulate with the flower.

Although in nature this specific insect-plant relationship makes cross pollination between different species uncommon, in cultivation it is an easy matter to remove pollinia and place them in contact with the stigma of any other orchid. It was soon discovered, as more orchids came into cultivation, that hybrids could be obtained, not only between species of the same genus but between different genera. Thus some of our modern cultivated kinds are the result of crossing one or more species from two, three, four or even more genera.

When two orchid genera are crossed the hybrid is known by a new generic name composed of parts of the names of the parent genera. Thus *Laelia* x *Cattleya* becomes *Laeliocattleya*. When more than two genera are involved either the same convention is employed, e.g. *Brassavola* x *Laelia* x *Cattleya* = *Brassolaeliocattleya* or to avoid such cumbersome names a new name is coined, always ending in *ara*. Thus *Brassavola* x *Cattleya* x *Laelia* x *Sophronitis* = *Potinara*. The progeny of any cross is given a hybrid or *grex* name and selected individuals, as no two seedlings will be exactly alike, are given a further *cultivar* name.

The first hybrids were grown by sowing the minute seeds, which will only germinate and grow in the presence of a certain fungus *(mycorrhiza)*, in the compost around one of the parent plants. Now, however, they are grown under sterile conditions in glass tubes on a specially formulated medium which contains substances which fulfil the function of the fungus.

Until relatively recently propagation of the unique cultivars could only be by division of the slow growing plants. Now by a process known as *meristem* culture a certain small part of the plant is removed, grown, and repeatedly divided, on a specially formulated medium. Each division will eventually produce a plant identical with the original.

Many orchids are not difficult to grow. Like any other cultivated plant all they require is the right combination of temperature, light and moisture and a suitable compost. A small heated greenhouse and a little know-how will enable anyone to grow many of the beautiful flowers depicted on the following pages.

Odontoglossum hybrid Crowborough *facing*.

Paphiopedilum Alcides *left,* an old primary hybrid.

Cymbidium hybrid *above.*

Brassolaeliocattleya hybrid *below left.*

Brassolaeliocattleya Seaforth Highlander *below right.*

A group of many kinds of orchids in cultivation at the Washington DC Botanical Gardens *overleaf.*

Laeliocattleya hybrid Lustrissima *above.*

Cattleya hybrid Oceanid *left,* a cross between *Cattleya* hybrid Nebo and *Cattleya* hybrid Trimos.

Sophrolaeliocattleya hybrid Kuma *below left,* a cross between *Cattleya trianaei,* a species from Colombia and *Sophrolaeliocattleya* hybrid Meuse.

Phalaenopsis hybrid Texas Star *top right.*

Cattleya lueddemanniana above, a species from Venezuela.

Phalaenopsis hybrid Inspiration *centre right.*

Gastrochilus acutifolius below, a species from the Himalayas.

Phalaenopsis hybrid Best Girl *bottom right.*

Phalaenopsis hybrid Roselle *left*.

Odontoglossum grande above, a species from Mexico.

Colax jugosus below, a species from Brazil.

Epidendrum vitellinum right, a species from Mexico.

Cymbidium hybrid *overleaf*, an example of a modern small flowered so called 'miniature' hybrid.

Cattleya bowringiana *above* and *below,* two different colour forms of a variable Central American species.

Lycaste hybrid Lucianii *left.*

Laelia anceps right, a species from Mexico.

Oncidium tigrinum above, a species from Mexico.

Oncidium ornithorhynchum top right, also from Mexico.

Oncidium hybrid centre right. Many hybrids in this very large genus have been raised in recent years.

Epidendrum ciliare far left, a species widespread in C. & S. America.

Cattleya schroederae left, a species from Colombia.

Laeliocattleya hybrid Bacchante *right,* a relatively recent hybrid between *Laeliocattleya* Berenice and *Cattleya* Dinah.

Phaius tankervilleae overleaf left, a commonly cultivated species from tropical Asia and Australia, and *Cymbidium* hybrid Bella *overleaf right,* a cross between *Cymbidium* hybrid Rusper and *Cymbidium* hybrid Ramboda.

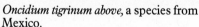

Oncidium excavatum above left, a species from S. America.

Ascocenda hybrid *above.*

Epidendrum fragrans below left, a widespread American species with the lip uppermost. This was one of the first tropical orchids to be cultivated in Europe.

Oncidium phymatochilum below, a species from Brazil.

Oncidium Barahona *right,* a recently produced hybrid.

Vanda hybrid *left.*

Phalaenopsis hybrid Viola Tanaka *above.*

Ludisia discolor below, a species from the Far East sometimes called jewel orchid.

Vanda merrillii right, a species from the Philippines.

Sophrolaelia hybrid Psyche *above left,* an artificial hybrid between the two species illustrated below.

Laelia cinnabarina centre left, a species from Brazil.

Sophronitis coccinea below left, a species from Brazil much utilised in hybridising for its brilliant red colour.

Coelogyne massangeana above, a species from the Far East.

Dendrobium x *delicatum below,* a natural hybrid *(Dendrobium speciosum* x *Dendrobium kingianum)* from Australia.

Polystachya pubescens right, a species from S. Africa.

Paphiopedilum hybrid Danella *left*, a typical modern slipper orchid with complex parentage.

Eria coronaria above, a species from India.

Paphiopedilum hybrid Constableanum *below*, a primary artificial hybrid (*Paphiopedilum fairieanum* x *Paphiopedilum dayanum*).

Odontoglossum uroskinneri right, a species from C. America.

Vanda hybrid Miss Joaquim *above left.* The first *Vanda* hybrid to be made.

Laelia pumila above, a species from Brazil.

Lycaste hybrid Jason below.

Laelia autumnalis right, a species from Mexico.

Dendrobium hybrid Ted Takiguchi *above and above left*, two views of the same inflorescence.

Brassolaeliocattleya hybrid Pure Gold *below left*.

Cattleya hybrid *below*.

Dendrobium hybrid *right, Dendrobium bigibbum* is the dominant species in the parentage of this artificial hybrid.

A group of cultivated hybrid *Phalaenopsis* hybrids *overleaf* (the plants with heart-shaped leaves bottom left are not orchids but anthuriums). The aerial roots of the orchids can be clearly seen.

Cattleya walkerana above, a species from Brazil.

Paphiopedilum hybrid Leyburnense *left.*

Dendrobium dearei right, a species from the Philippines.

Angraecum compactum below, a species from Madagascar.

Paphiopedilum hybrid Wynnetta *overleaf.* A cross between *Paphiopedilum* hybrid Wynnetta Puddle and *Paphiopedilum* hybrid Chianti.

Sophrolaelia hybrid Affric *left*. The red *Sophronitis* colour is dominant in this cross.

Odontioda hybrid Keighliensis 'Craybrooke' *above*.

Masdevallia veitchiana below, the specific name is in honour of James Veitch, a famous 19th century orchid grower. A species from Peru.

Sophrolaelia hybrid Jewel Box 'Fairy Ring' *right*.

Odontoglossum rossii top left, a species from C. America.

Masdevallia schroederana centre left, a species from Peru. The large colourful part of the flower is in this genus not the lip, which is very small, but the two lateral sepals joined together.

Cattleya leopoldii bottom left, a species from Brazil.

Miltonia clowesii above, a species from Brazil.

Cymbidium dayanum below, a species from the Far East named in honour of John Day, a famous 19th century grower and painter of orchids who flowered it for the first time in 1868.

Epidendrum hybrid Orchidglade *right*. The hybrid name is that of the American orchid nursery where the plant was first raised.

Phalaenopsis schillerana overleaf, a species from the Philippines. Many of the modern *Phalaenopsis* hybrids have been derived from this species.

Phalaenopsis hybrid Rainbow Falls *left*. The name *Phalaenopsis* is derived from *Phalaena*, a moth, and members of the genus are sometimes called moth orchids.

Dendrobium hybrid Golden Wave 'Number One' *above*.

Vanda hybrid *top right*.

Oncidium papilio below, a species from S. America.

Oncidium species *centre right*.

Vanda hybrid *bottom*.

Cattleya hybrid Half Moon Bay *bottom right*.

Miltonia hybrid Brugendres *above*. Hybrids of this type are sometimes called pansy orchids.

Oeceoclades ugandae left, a rare species from Uganda.

Masdevallia coccinea below, a species from Colombia. The genus produces some of the most brilliant colours in the family.

Doritis pulcherrima right, a species from tropical Asia.

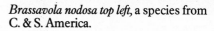

Brassavola nodosa top left, a species from C. & S. America.

Brassavola cucullata above, another species from the same region.

Coelogyne fimbriata centre left, a species from tropical Asia.

Scuticaria hadwenii bottom left, a species from Brazil.

Masdevallia hybrid *measureseana below*.

Masdevallia tovarensis right, a species from Venezuela.

Vuylstekeara hybrid Edna *left*, a cross involving the genera *Cochlioda, Miltonia* and *Odontoglossum*.

Masdevallia hybrid Kimballiana *above*.

Phalaenopsis violacea above right, a very variable species from tropical Asia.

Cochlioda rosea below, a species from Peru and Ecuador.

Sophronitis cernua below right, a species from Brazil.

Vanda merrillii above, a species from the Philippines named in honour of the famous American botanist E.D. Merrill.

Dendrobium hybrid Tomie *left.*

Phalaenopsis hybrids *below and right.*

Dendrobium hybrid Princess Sharon *left.* *Dendrobium* hybrids have become very popular in recent years but need really warm conditions to grow well.

Phalaenopsis hybrid, details of the lip and column of the hybrid shown *on page 53* from the side *above* and from the front *below.*

Cattleya alliance hybrids, *top, centre and below right.*

Barkeria lindleyana left, a species from C. America. Named after the great orchidologist John Lindley.

Oncidium hybrid Kaiulani *above,* a cross between *Oncidium flexuosum* and *Oncidium ornithorhynchum.*

Oncidium excavatum below, a species from S. America.

Oncidium altissimum right, a species from C. & S. America.

Gomesa crispa *top left*, a species from Brazil.

Laeliocattleya hybrid Bowri-albida *above*, a cross between *Laelia albida* and *Cattleya bowringiana*.

Potinara hybrid Gorgeous Star *centre left*, a cross between four genera, *Brassavola*, *Cattleya*, *Laelia* and *Sophronitis*.

Cymbidium dayanum bottom left, a species from the Far East.

Doritaenopsis hybrid Jerry Vande Weghe *below*, a cross between *Doritis* and *Phalaenopsis*.

Paphiopedilum hybrid White Hart *right*. *Paphiopedilum* hybrids are very popular as they are relatively easy to grow and have long lasting flowers.

Phalaenopsis hybrid Richard Schaeffer *above.*

Vanda hybrid *left and below.* Vandas need rather hot conditions to grow well.

Vanda hybrid *right.*

Spathoglottis plicata left, a species from the Far East.

Phalaenopsis amabilis above, a species from the Far East.

Cymbidium miniature hybrid *right.*

Vanda hybrid *above.*

Phaius tankervilleae below growing wild in the Philippines.

Cattleya hybrid *right.*

First published in Great Britain 1979 by Colour Library International Ltd.
© Illustrations: Colour Library International (U.S.A.) Ltd, 163 East 64th Street, New York 10021.
Colour separations by Fercrom, Barcelona, Spain.
Display and text filmsetting by Focus Photoset, London, England.
Printed and bound by L.E.G.O.– Vicenza – Italy.
Published by Crescent Books, a division of Crown Publishers Inc.
All rights reserved.
Library of Congress Catalogue Card No. 78-72002
CRESCENT 1979